Your Own Course and Final Destiny

Your Own Course and Final Destiny

Table Of Contents

Foreword

"It is not in the stars to hold our destiny but in ourselves." ~ William Shakespeare

Are you the one who controls your life or is your life controlling you? Which road should you take? Do you know which path will lead you to where you really want to be?

Creating and shaping your own destiny is one of the many things that only a handful of persons can successfully do, while most end up aimlessly cruising through life, hoping that one day, their predetermined fate will step in and lady luck will shine on their lives.

If you want to live with purpose, the first thing that you have to do is to know remember that more than anyone or anything else, it is only you who have the sole power of creating the destiny that you have defined. It is you who have the ability of preparing for the opportunities that are bound to come your way. It is you who make things happen. You do not just put your trust on fate. Creating your own path and destiny is actually all up to you. That is the foremost thing that you need to keep in mind if you really want to live a life with purpose. Get all the info you need here.

Your Own Path And Destiny

Chapter 1:

Living On Purpose Basics

Synopsis

"You were put on this earth to achieve your greatest self, to live out your purpose, and to do it fearlessly." ~ Steve Maraboli

Most people today are struggling with the concern that how they are doing their lives is not really in sync with living their life's purpose. But what are the basics of living on purpose? How will you be able to live a life that is aligned with your calling, authentic and put into action your purpose every single day?

The Basics

Awareness

First, you have to be aware that "what is" is not necessarily the genuine expression of your creative, powerful and true self. You have to begin acknowledging the difference of being mindful of how you live in today, the present moment, and how you constantly project your personal desires in the future which have chances of not turning out real.

Be Committed

Show your commitment on working on this present path, made more interesting by the unconscious impulses and discover what it really takes to conquer reactivity. Learn to live intentionally and start expressing the real you.

Search for Guidance

To find a new direction, you need to search for proper guidance and gain support for new learning for it is only through this that you will get to discover the authenticity of your life.

Go for Clarity

Living on purpose requires you to be clear about your own personality. You need to know what values you uphold and identify your passions, strengths and weaknesses, all of which should be aligned as you claim your life's purpose together with the intention of serving greater good and meeting humanity's needs.

Render Service

The highest form of life fulfillment stems from serving those around you, driven by your desire to express your purpose after you have finally known your inner self.

Take a Step Forward

Commit yourself to your brand new path of living on purpose today and step forward as you create a plan on how to you further develop yourself to become better tomorrow.

Be Thankful

At the end of the day, living your life's purpose boils down on saying thank you and being grateful for being alive, with all the chances of experiencing energy, breath and all of the basic goodness of life.

Chapter 2:

Figuring Out What You Want Your Life To Look Like

Synopsis

Everybody wants the ideal life. Everyone dreams of getting through all the hoops, being glorious and becoming happy in the easiest way possible. However, before you actually make all of your dreams come true, it is important that you first figure out what you really want your life to look like. What are the things that you can do to get there, wherever "there" might be?

What You Want

In reality, most people want all of the best things in life, but more often than not, they fail to do much for them to get started with their life's actual journey. Simply put, many people are stuck behind their lives' wheels, unmoving, and worse, there are some who just sit comfortably in the back seat as they let another person navigate their own lives.

You are the one who makes your own life, not anybody else, and for you to determine what it will look like in the future, you should start with today, because it is in the present that you would really be able to set what your life would be like 20 or even 50 years from now.

So, how should you get started?

Stop Wondering About the Things That You Want – Figure Things Out Today

For all you know, you are probably not even aware of how you want your life to be or look like. Think about this: When was the last time that you sat down while introspecting and searching for your soul to figure out the things that you want? Has it been awhile?

Soul searching is the best ticket for you to understand how and what you want your life to look like, so make sure that you set aside some of your time for it. When you finally understand what you actually want, this can bring you more happiness and make you feel more fulfilled, something that everyone will surely wish to have.

Set Goals Outside the Boundaries of Your Comfort Zone

What's the sense of taking a journey if you will not take risks and be bold in the steps that you take? Well, this does not necessarily mean that you need to do dangerous or irresponsible things. What it means is that you have to be more daring, more ambitious and unafraid. You must be fearless and brave in facing your goals, with the determination that you can achieve more out of your life. And to start this, you should set goals that are way beyond your comfort zone.

Muster Up Confidence That Will Drive You Into Action

Confidence is the primary ingredient that is bound to drive you into full-swing action. You will discover that when you have gained more confidence to help you reach your bold goals, you will also be able to set aside all your vulnerabilities and fears. With more conviction intact, you will soon discover more strategies that can fill in the gaps in your confidence which kept you into being a passenger right inside the vehicle of your life.

Be in Charge and Do the Needed Work

Whether you like it or not, the work should be done by you and you alone. No one will do it for you so unless you take action, you will never be able to figure out what your life would be like. Get up and run your life towards the direction that you want it to take. Seize every chance and opportunity thrown your way and find and create the happiness of your life. After all, living on purpose means taking charge, getting out and being the own driver of your life, before anything else.

Chapter 3:

Making Goals And Sticking To Them

Synopsis

Now that you have your life all figured out, the next thing that you need to do is set your goals and learn how you should stick to them. Most people, when setting their goals, imagine a simple and straight path towards their destination.

However, the sad truth is that the path to reaching your goals is hardly ever linear and clear.

This path has lots of obstacles and expecting to find a linear and straight path will surely derail you even before you start. On the contrary, anticipating obstacles will help you in conquering them more easily than what you have expected.

Goals

Forget Your Doubts and Never Overthink

Once you have set a plan which you are sure will work, sticking to it can be all too easy. Yet the moment doubt starts creeping in, you will get a change in behavior and ironically enough, this very change is what will wreck the whole plan.

Although doubt can sometimes has its good side as it will make you think twice prior to continuing the thing that you do, you need to remember that the right place and time for doubts is during planning stages only.

Once you are in the middle of taking action, doubts no longer have their place. Choose one path and make sure that you follow through it until you reached success or that predetermined evaluation point.

Put Aside Resources For Them Not to Run Out

The most common excuses that people have when they fail to do something that they should be doing include lack of energy, lack of time, and of course, lack of money.

Sources like these are finite and once they have not been allocated properly, expect to run out of them. When you make goals, you must determine the one that has more chances of becoming your excuse and search for a means for it not to hinder your way. Create a schedule, do the things that are more important first, or set aside some funds.

Define Your Priorities to Resist the Shiny Objects

In life, even after you have set all your goals and become determined to reach them, there will always come a time when your priorities suddenly take a sudden shift. There was probably one time when your goal was the most essential thing to you yet once an unexpected incidence takes place, this goal becomes completely abandoned as you deal with your latest predicament. However, the million dollar question is, was it all worth it? How many chances did you lose when you stopped persisting? Did you ever wish to go back and continued on instead? Make sure that you weigh things properly in order for you not to feel any regrets in the end.

Stay Right on Track by Reaffirming Habits

To reach and stick to your goals, your habits play a crucial role. It is true that the easiest means of accomplishing something which requires effort for a certain time period is through creating behavioral routines as you reach all your goals. But what if a certain situation arises and the whole momentum gets disrupted? Start from the very beginning: first, change your emotions before changing your behavior. Rekindle your original motivation which pushed you to setting that particular goal then proceed to reestablishing your habit.

Chapter 4:

How Living On Purpose Works

Synopsis

"The purpose of life is not to be happy. It is to be useful, to be honorable, to be compassionate, to have it make some difference that you have lived and lived well." ~Ralph Waldo Emerson

Have you reached that point when confusions, yearnings, emptiness, depression, and the lacking feeling all merged together? And what's even worse is when they present themselves during those times when you feel like the whole world is on your shoulders?

How It Happens

The simple things, just like getting out your bed each morning, feel so heavy and life's best joys, such as making new friends and spending time with your family, become unsatisfying. Things feel hard, heavy, to the point that they are unbearable.

BUT, before you crumble on your feet, you need to know that there is still a way for your life to transform, and that is by learning how to live on purpose.

On the first few chapters, you have learned about the basics of living on purpose, knowing how you want your life to look like, and how you should make and stick to your goals. In this chapter, you will know how living on purpose really works.

Before anything else, you need first to know the various kinds of types. When you live a practical life of purpose, there is the so-called "macro" level and "micro" level.

For micro level purpose, this is when you know all your values and you start integrating with them. Once you know what it is really that you stand for then you do whatever it is you believe it, your sense of self-worth and confidence will also skyrocket, even though the situation might suck.

But it is only a small aspect of living on purpose.

As for the macro level, this is an entirely different thing.

This time, this is the larger picture.

This is when you search for your meaning. This is your one ultimate goal.

This is when you wake up every morning, knowing that you are on the path where you want to be, no matter what others might say.

To know how to live on purpose, you need to know the missing piece that will complete the puzzle. What is this piece? It is discovering that your ultimate purpose is to give, not to get.

Everyone ones better for themselves and for their lives, but purpose – such as happiness and success – is in truth, counterintuitive.

You must never aim at success for the more that you do it and consider it your target, the more chances that you will actually miss it. Success such as happiness, is not something to be pursued. This must ensue. If you want money, help others make money! If you want others to love you, love others first!

And once you have done this, once you have become of service to others, this is when everything comes together, and you finally find yourself, when you finally know what living on purpose is really all about.

Chapter 5:

Synopsis

Having the right mindset is so powerful that it is important for you to be able to live your life on purpose. But how do you get the right mindset? The answer is simple – you just need to be positive!

If you will be asked to listen to all your thoughts, are you going to say that majority of them are negative or positive?

Things You Have To Know

Shockingly, the most destructive source of all the negativities in your life is yourself. Most people are being bombarded by different negative thoughts and the truth is, thinking in the negative is way much easier than thinking on a positive term simply because every single day, we are getting a lot of negative messages, both externally and internally, such as those news on the media.

The real problem starts once your mind accepts these negatives as the truth. You focus on your problems and spend a lot of hours each day predicting the bad news for yourselves, and this will then generate worry, confusion, and fear.

However, in reality, thinking positively does not really call for extra effort. You can have all the negative messages filtered out by simply focusing on those positive things in your life. The first step you need to take to have positive thoughts replace the negative ones is making the decision, something that is easier once you are constantly reminded of the benefits that this will inflict into your life.

When you have a positive mindset, not only you but the whole world can become so much better. With positive thoughts, these can serve as s solid shield that will protect your dreams and yourself from all negative things around you. In addition, positive thinking also makes you feel better, both physically and mentally.

To get in the right positive mindset and attitude, you need to be confident and self-assured. Focus on your positive aspects. Know your exceptional strengths, determine the things that you have successfully accomplished. Be confident in being aware that change will help you grow and it will then help in boosting your self-esteem, and finally, believe that you can really make that much coveted change!

Handling problems can become easier when you do not give negative thoughts a chance of taking control over yourself and how you feel towards life. See to it that you have positive expectations each day and in your life as a whole.

Come up with healthier decisions by looking at the whole picture. And lastly, be passionate about the goals that you have in life. Let them serve as your encouragement of persevering over the obstacles. The determination to meet a goal, small or big it might be, can strengthen your self-esteem and confidence.

Getting in the right mindset might not be easy but when you surround yourself only with positive thoughts, even the most negative things that life throws your way will never knock you down, whatever happens.

Take time in reflecting things and be always on the lookout for brand new chances. Learn the lessons that you need to learn and take a step forward with more confidence.

Chapter 6:

The Difference Between Positive And Negative Mindset In Creating Your Path

Synopsis

You have already learned that getting in the right mindset will require you to be more positive in your life.

However, do you know that there is more to positive thinking than just what you can see on the surface?

Based on research, it has been discovered that positive thinking is way beyond than simply being happy or showing the upbeat attitude.

With positive thoughts and mindset, you will be able to give more value to your life, helping you create your rightful path as you build skills which can last way much longer compared to a simple smile.

The Differences

Negative Thoughts – Your Brain's Wrecking Ball

Say you are walking alone in the woods and all of a sudden, a tiger shows up from nowhere right in front of you. Right at that moment, one negative emotion registers in your brain – fear.

It has long been discovered by researchers that your brain is being programmed by your negative emotions to make a particular action. For instance, when the tiger takes one step towards you, you just run. You forget about the world, because your thoughts are focused on that tiger alone, the fear it ignites in you, and how you will be able to escape from it.

Simply put, negative emotions can focus your thoughts, narrowing your mind at the same time. You always have the choice to look for a high tree that you can climb or you can look for a stick to serve as your weapon but these options are all irrelevant because all you can think about is that a tiger is right there in front of you.

While such a scenario no longer happens in today's society, your brain still responds to negative emotions in this very way – with the whole world shut off and you see only a limited number of options around you.

Well, it can be safe to say that a negative mindset is the wrecking ball of your brain. As you create your path and try to shape your destiny, your negative thoughts will impede you from discovering more about the world around you and when this happens, you will not be able to see all of the choices that you've got.

Positive Mindset – Your Brain's Power

A positive mindset does not simply stop once good feelings start subsiding. In reality, the most important benefit that you can get from having a positive mindset is the enhanced ability of building skills and developing resources which you can use later on in your life.

Your positive emotions will open up your mind and widen your sense of possibilities and this will then allow you to create new resources and skills which can give value to other aspects of your life.

In creating your own path, positive and negative mindsets do exactly the opposite. If you want your life to become better and you want a path that leads you to where you would want to be, all it takes is to have a positive mindset to get you there.

Chapter 7:

How Important Is It To Stick With It

Synopsis

Why do you need to stick with your positive mindset? There is no denying that positive thinking is something that does not come naturally to a person but there are actually a lot of reasons why you must now start in cultivating positive thoughts and lessen the negative ideas running around your mind.

The Importance

Better Way to Cope with Stress

Living your life's purpose is not always an easy thing and stressful situations will arise no matter how much you try to stay away from them. When you are a positive think, you can cope with these stress factors much better and more effectively compared to the pessimists. While pessimists tend to take problems as something that they cannot change, optimists will more likely come up with an action plan and call for advice and assistance from others for the issue to be resolved.

Enhance Your Immunity with Optimism

It has been recently discovered that a person's mind can have a powerful impact on one's body. If there is one area which can be greatly influenced by your attitudes and thoughts, that would be your immunity. Based on one study, when negative emotions are activated in the brain, a person's immune response to flu vaccine tends to be weaker. It was discovered that people who are positive about a crucial and particular area of their lives, like how they perform at work, showed a much stronger immune response as compared to the ones who nurse negative thoughts regarding the situation.

Improve Your Health with Positive Thoughts

A positive mind will not just improve your immunity and ability of coping with stress. At the same time, this will affect your entire well-being. Experts associated several health benefits with optimism, which include less depression, reduced chances of death caused by cardiovascular issues and increased lifespan. Even though it is still unclear how positive thinking can benefit the health of a person, some say that people who nurse positive thoughts are the ones who follow a healthier lifestyle. As they cope better with stress and avoid unhealthy behaviors, they also improve their well being and health.

Resiliency Made Possible by a Positive Mind

Being resilient means having the ability of coping with problems. People who manifest resiliency are the ones who can face a trauma or crisis with better resolve and strength.

They do not fall apart when stress comes their way and instead, they carry on, eventually overcoming the adversity. It is no longer surprising that resiliency is greatly affected by positive thinking. As mentioned earlier, optimists look for ways on how to fix an issue when faced with a challenge.

They do not give up hope and instead, they marshal the available resources and never have any qualms of asking for others' help.

Sticking to a positive mindset is very important for it is through this will you be able to create the path that you want.

Chapter 8:

How To Make Things Happen

Synopsis

"The thing about life is that you must survive. Life is going to be difficult, and dreadful things will happen. What you do is move along, get on with it, and be tough.

Not in the sense of being mean to others, but being tough with yourself and making a deadly effort not to be defeated." ~Katharine Hepburn

Making things happen is not as easy as it may seem. Yes, you can always devise a plan, and yes, you can always get in the right positive mindset that will help you throughout your journey in the path that you choose.

However, there are some things that you need to do just so you can be sure that whatever you have conceived in your mind will really push through.

How To

First of all, you have to remember that everyone, and that includes you, deserve unconditionally love, miracles and creation, simply because you are among God's perfect creations.

To make things happen, finding some quiet time for yourself will also be of great help. Every single day, the lives of the people are cluttered by different sounds that it might be a bit hard to listen to that voice coming from deep within.

Most have already lost connection with their inner soul that they end up clueless of their true desires. Allot a few minutes of your day to some soul searching and expect to get the much needed help for making things happen.

While your past still plays a big role in your present, it does not mean that you have to be imprisoned there for the rest of your life. Let bygones be bygones.

Decide for your now, this moment, and start to create what you really want for your life. There is no need for you to ask for the permission or approval of anyone around you to do it.

As mentioned in the earlier chapters, setting your goals is very important because how can you make things happen when you do not know what these "things" are? Determine the things that you want for your life, the things that can bring joy to your being while still ensuring that you serve others along the way.

Take note that to make things happen and for you to fulfill your life's purpose, you need to focus more on today. As the old saying goes, it is called "present" because the "now" is a gift.

Be patient and learn to love yourself as you take your journey towards discovering your true power. Stay attuned to everything around you and when you do just that, things will start unfolding all by themselves.

Chapter 9:
Advantages and Disadvantages

Synopsis

How you see your life is what shapes your life. When you live with purpose, when you take the necessary steps to creating your own path and destiny, you are actually creating exactly the kind of life that you want for yourself. And while it is said that everything in this earth comes with their positives and negatives, living on purpose is more of advantages and benefits. There is nothing bad about it.

Good And Bad

The Beauty of Living on Purpose

When you know your purpose, you actually give your life with meaning. Everyone is created with meaning, and it is the very reason why through the centuries, people have been trying dubious methods just to discover what this meaning is. If you know the meaning of your life, you will be able to bear just about anything. With no meaning, everything will become unbearable.

Knowing what your purpose is will simplify your life. It will define the things that you do and do not do. This very purpose is what will become your standard in evaluating the essential and unessential activities in your life.

If you have no clear or definite purpose, you will lack the foundation where you will base your decisions, use your resources, and allocate your time.

The tendency is for you to make your choices depending on that moment's pressures, circumstances, and your mood. When you do not know what your purpose is, you will end up doing too much, which will then cause fatigue, stress, and worse, conflict.

Your life will also become more focused when you know your purpose. It will help concentrate your energy and effort on the most important things. This way, you will become more effective as you start being selective.

As you start to learn what your purpose is, you will also become motivated, as purpose produces passion. A clear purpose will energize you and fire you up. Waking up in the morning will no longer be a major chore and going to the office will no longer wear you down and sap you of your strength and rob you of your life's joys.

Chapter 10:

Conclusion

Synopsis

"The only person you are destined to become is the person you decide to be." ~Ralph Waldo Emerson

No one else steers the wheel of your life. At the end of the day, you are the captain of your own journey. You call the shots. You are the one who makes the decisions, not other people. It is you who decides which road to take, which path you should follow. It is you who picks from the cards that you are dealt with. It is you who creates your life.

To know the purpose of your life is wonderful, for it is true this knowledge that you actually get the inspiration that you need to pursue the kind of life that you want for yourself. You start with figuring out what you want your life to look like. Once you have envisioned that life, you then proceed to making your goals. And it is not enough that you only make goals. You need to stick to them. You need to make sure that you will achieve all of them. How do you do it? Simple, you just need to get in the right mindset. You need to be more positive and nurse only positive emotions and thoughts for any negativity will surely stop you in your track, probably even before you start.

If you think that your life is now swerving into the wrong direction, it is about time that you start getting back on the path that you chose for yourself. While there is nothing wrong with believing that your story has already been written in a book somewhere and things will just go as planned, wouldn't it be better if you are the one who creates your destiny? Would it not be even more exciting to know that everything good that will happen in the future will be the results of your right actions and decisions today? Would it not be more fulfilling on your part to know that your success in the future is actually the product of your perseverance and determination at present?

To life a life fully, you need to live a life that you created yourself. This way, there will be no regrets, no pointing of fingers, and no disappointments. This way, you can say that even though there might be failures along the way, at least, you did what you need to do and no one dictated you to do things that you do not want to do.

Create your own destiny! Find the path that you want for your life! Start living your life today!

"No matter what your history has been, your destiny is what you create today. What are you going to create?" ~Steve Maraboli